BONE LANGUAGE

BONE LANGUAGE

JAMAICA

BALDWIN

YESYES BOOKS

Cover art: *Zvandiswededza (It Has Drawn Me Closer)*, 2017, © Portia Zvavahera
Oil-based printing ink and oil bar on canvas, 172 × 168 cm
Courtesy of Stevenson and David Zwirner
Photo: Mario Todeschini
Cover & Interior Design: Alban Fischer
Project Lead: KMA Sullivan

ISBN 978-1-936919-94-9
Printed in the United States of America

Published by YesYes Books
1631 NE Broadway St #121
Portland, OR 97232
yesyesbooks.com

KMA Sullivan, Publisher
Joanna Acevedo, Assistant Editor
Alban Fischer, Graphic Designer
A. Tony Jerome, Assistant Editor
Karah Kemmerly, Assistant Editor
Jill Kolongowski, Manuscript Copy Editor
James Sullivan, Assistant Editor, Audio Books
Gale Marie Thompson, Senior Editor, Book Development

CONTENTS

III.

for my mother

Without you my air tastes
like nothing. For you
I hold my breath.

—MARY SZYBIST

I.

I want to know what survives, what's handed down
from mother to daughter, if anything is,
bond I cannot cut away, that keeps apart what it lashes together.

—SUJI KWOK KIM

THE MESS A BODY MAKES

My mother offered me her history
licking the fat off each gristled story,
her fingers shiny with the destruction
of her youth. I followed carefully behind
consuming the world with unwritten poems
sewed into the hem of my dress,
a dull razor tucked beneath my tongue.
At the clearing in the woods, I built a church
out of the tender violence of words.

*

I wallow at the altar and worship
the mess a body makes barricaded
inside its own hailstorm of hunger.
I never learned how to pray but perhaps
the animal body is all I need in the end.
Perhaps when my words inevitably fail
I will open my mouth wide only to close it
again, to bite down hard one last time,
to gnaw the bone, to lick the red language
from my fingers, glistening.

BORROWED HONEY

Once, mother, I too writhed in the pale
gold afternoon honeyed with longing,

the shunt of my desire quickening
into currency the way I quickened into boys;

boys were what I learned to love about myself,
how quench I could become.

I kept tightening my grip, kept secrets
from coughing up blue and sex

I kept at bay till it moored me with hunger.
I unfastened from myself waiting for you,

who kept afternooning inside sleep's memory,
who kept memoring inside anti-depressant afternoons.

Again and again I found you napping on a bed
shattered with the words of dead women:

(Plath, Sexton, Woolf).
I began listening to nude songs on repeat

till a boy wrapped them in yellow and sat them
by the fire; he wouldn't listen when I told him

melancholy is its own kind of heat.
I couldn't green without shame but all I wanted

was a love that desired me anyway, or anyway,
at least someone that loved my desire,

which is to say, mother, I don't begrudge you
your colors, which is to say, I kept answering

your drowned voice with my own, kept singing
along to our borrowed honey, kept words—

the dead of women, quick with longing.

SEEING IN THE DARK

When I was twelve, I learned Morse code. Spent a weekend
at Pidgeon Point Lighthouse with a ham radio, tapping greetings
to kids in Russia then waiting for their response in return.
Now, when I think of lighthouses, I think of us eager to reach across
borders, or that Sinéad O'Connor song about the woman forever
waiting for her man to return from sea. And sometimes I'm the woman
alone in a lighthouse with underwater memories, always waiting.
Some nights, I search my body with a flashlight for signs of a future.

Light, we've been taught, is how we find each other in the dark,
the omnidirectional lens guiding boats away from dangerous edges,
the North Star, the moonlight: a point of reference to cling to
in the dark emptiness of night.   Dark.   Empty.
The language they ascribe to our bodies is made of the same shadow
and warning. It's no wonder they fear us, no wonder my father
at sixty-three was a miracle, no wonder night, like his body, has been
riddled with the language of dread. But light isn't the surest way home.
We've grown accustomed to the ease of it, as if ease was the point
of living, grown idle in our new skins, forgetting our nocturnal ways.

Every now and then I remember what it felt like to see in the dark
beyond what the light reveals, to see how perfect we all are
in the absence of its confident gaze. I've never seen a night unpolluted
by light, never loved a body that wasn't held up to light's scrutiny,
but I'm learning. Last night I ate in the dark. Closed the blackout
curtains and touched my body in new ways. I remembered to be grateful.

I remembered what Toni Morrison said about impenetrable whiteness,
that such allusions are sinister and lazy. I remember that shadow is only
ominous because language made it so. I swear to you, listening
to Nina Simone in the assiduous dark will shatter you on a cellular level.

This is the ocean of what we've lost inscribed in night's unfolding,
not an eke, but a bellow, a darkness so rapturous it blinds.

NEGLECTUS

1. a raven whispers his Black
   to the tree living amidst
   the rubble of burned forest

   the tree whispers back in
   voices of the recently deceased

   we have heard our twinned night
   our oil-feathered beast cry
   there is a war happening

2. a negligible amount of toxins
    is allowed in our food   on our bodies

    a negligible amount of death
    is allowed in the Black population

    negligible

    from the Latin neglectus, past participle of neglegere
    to make light of, disregard, be indifferent to, not heed, not trouble oneself about

    literally

    not to pick up

                        these bodies are not to be picked up
                        attended to
                        kissed
                        where it hurts
                        allowed to hurt
                        feel
                        yearn
                        desire
                        love

3.   inside a bird box a rough hand
covers the mouth of its lover

inside the child hides
between the teeth of her mother's fantasies
to escape the toxins of war

and the mother opens her mouth
and parts her lips
and sound spills like blood from between her legs

4. i want to turn power over in my hands   to feel
    its rough edges

    this substance grafted from fear   layers and layers
    worked and reworked

    till it appears smooth and shiny
    till it appears like something worth dying for

FILM SCRIPT:
ON THE OPEN ROAD
(AN ANTI-DRAMA)

It troubles me to think of death, not the
last breath hell-bent on one final note
but the aftermath that those who come close
claim is a bleached white expanse of endless
light. I don't take comfort in this. I prefer
to think of my father surrounded by
a luxurious darkness, chocolate
bougainvilleas, molten glass, silk sounds of
Marvin Gaye or Pendergrass. I see him
on his Harley, riding at cruise speed, tires
churning rocks into rain behind him. There
are no speeding tickets there. No police.
No alcoholism. Just a Black man. And
an open road without a destination.

TEACHING THE BEASTS TO DEVOUR MY MOTHER

When we talk casually about death,
    my mother tells me she doesn't want anything
burned or buried, nothing stuffed,
    painted or preserved, nothing dressed up
pretty or folded neatly into prayer.

        What do you want then? I ask. She smiles.
           Says, *fly me over the densest forest.*
        Push me quick and let the animals have at me,
           let my last act be amends, my body of use,
        let the vultures pick up the pieces and give me flight.

I don't think that's legal, I say.
    And she tells me that's my problem.
I don't think that's legal, I said
    as if laws were my only hesitation, as if
I wouldn't wander the woods searching

for the madwoman living in trees, speaking
in tongues. As if I could ever believe she was gone.
When she lands all thud and broken
and lung spent. When her eyes have settled
permanently on the sun stretching its jealous fingers

through leaves and memory, I will ask
the circling beasts to leave her toes their kingdom
a while longer, to let them grip the earth
to feel it shudder, let her arms gesticulate
a post-mortem map, a topographical salutation

(those exuberant exaggerations that once shamed
my teenage cheeks red). Who was I
to attempt to pin down her wingful ways?
That perpetual hippie sitting on the sidewalk.
Her legs spread out in front of her like tarot cards.

Her bare blackened feet, a callused *fuck you!*
to the establishment of keep-your-legs-crossed.
Her hairy legs grinning toward freedom
in her long patchwork skirt, speaking sideways
to trees, bumming cigarettes off older men,

swapping spit from a bottle of Rossi passed
        between friends. My mother wasn't a deadhead
kind of hippie but a soon-to-be-scuffing-the-disco
        floor-in-Candies-to-Cameo kind of hippie,
an I-don't-believe-in-Jerry-any-more-than-

I-believe-in-sin kind of hippie. But
        she memorized the scriptures of the unshaven,
the braless, scoffed at all things lady and decent.
        She cursed like a hangover and slept like a semi.
I wish I could have seen it: that time

        she streaked her hometown parade
            on a dare at 16, her long blonde hair whipping
        the air into frenzy, the town sheriff laughing at her
            rebellious bounce and jiggle. My mother kissed risk
        with red glossed lips and Camel cigs.

I was thrice almost blinded by these
        careless consumptions. Sometimes what I see
dissolves in front of me as if my bull's eyes were misses,
        as if my love lives were elegy, as if
I've simply waded through this one and only life.

But this is how a life unfolds when you're taught
          to dream by an owl, hibernate in summertime
and drink anything put in front of you
          as if it were your last hallelujah. So, to the beasts
who will one day devour my mother, I say,

wait until the forest is drunk with moon
          and windsong, until the insects have rustled
leaves into slow dance. Wait until her body
          loosens its grip and remembers how it felt to wander
wild and wingful.

ALL THAT SPLENDOR

after Vievee Francis

I watch them work, spiders
with their trapeze swings,
spinning worlds so easily broken
by the avalanche of my body.

This breaking of webs
isn't always an accident. No.
Sometimes I just want to ruin something perfect,
to see how quickly it bounces back.
      Tell me
you haven't wanted to tarnish, to dull
all that ferocious effort.

Tell me you haven't been stretched and left
delicate, barely there,
till every part of you is an entrance.

This is what happens when we leave
all our splendor out in the open,
slivers of translucent shimmers
just begging to be pulled apart.

II.

Lily open too wide too soon, bending sunward
at an angle nothing living should have to.

—CARL PHILLIPS

FORBIDDEN

Let me go back to my father
in the body of my mother the day he told her
having black children won't save you when the revolution comes.
Let me do more than laugh
like she did.

Let me go back to my mother
and do more
than roll my eyes when she tells me,
I think deep down, in a past life, I was a black blues singer.

My mother remembers the convent
where she worked after I was born;
the nuns who played with me while she cleaned.

My father remembers the bedroom window
of their first apartment, his tired body
climbing through. It was best,

they agreed, if she signed the lease alone.

Scholars conclude
the myths of violence that surround the black male
body protect the white female

from harm. I conclude
race was indeed a factor in my parents' attraction.
I am the product of their curiosity, their vengeance, their need.

They rescued each other from stories scripted
onto their bodies. They tasted forbidden and devoured each other
whole.

Let me build a house
where their memories diverge.

Let me lick clean
these bones.

BONELESS

My father was de-boned as a child.
The trick was to use a sharp knife,
steady hands and always begin at the neck.
With luck, my grandparents
were able to remove his spine intact.

But all-muscle can't hold love upright.
Strength needs something to settle itself
around. You see, boneless men
can only stay where they are bent to.
My father was made to cut

his own beatings off a tree.
Like pentimenti I sometimes see through
his scars: a perfect whole. But you can't
dream the broken out of a person
no matter how hard you try.

FAR FROM GRACE

I learned mothers can devour their young
in their sleep.

I learned bourbon brings grit to my mother's laughter
and slumbering lions should not be woken

ever.

Mom said, it's not depression,
it's freedom.

I said, yes, but even freedom takes less
than three hours to get out of bed.

When I was learning to read, my mother
taped words to things she thought I should know:

door, chair, mirror,
closet, sink, refrigerator.

I taped words to her in return:

sleeping, don't disturb,
crying, quiet, I'm sorry.

We speak the same language now.

When I try to reach her
I no longer cut my tongue on her sadness.

THE END OF SORROW IS NOT HAPPINESS

I've gained many things since cancer: poetry, extra
weight, a distrust of happiness—the way this country
names it a pursuit, a destination most are never meant
to reach no matter how many shovels we break digging
there is always more earth, more history, more heft
required to fail. Even if I could make my way through
their labyrinth of promises without coming undone
I'm not sure I'd want to give up my sorrows, all my
reckless patients wandering through untamed hallways.
I've grown accustomed to their defiance, to the melancholy
of women unbolting private alienations. I prefer this
fracture of a home we've built together without borders,
without hustle. And the birds pay us no mind here,
nor the trees, nor moss. So much endless brilliant moss.

WHAT REMAINS

I don't remember much
before my mother got sober.

She tells me she wasn't around
all the time, by which she meant
she can't confirm who touched
or was touched by my body.

      I imagine
      those early years full of daggers and dandelions:
      sharp cuts that separate and drift
      into the air of me when I touched them.

Sanity can be like that:
a coat of paint on a subway train,
something beige and simple
we put over the bright graffiti, over all

the years of dirt and grease and blood, over all
the people within screaming
their existence onto trains, shaking
spray cans till the pressure builds and builds and explodes
into something vibrant.

Unmistakable.

AFTER THE MOTHER HAS MADE AMENDS AND GONE TO BED

Brother, you were born seven years later, greening from earth
like moss, clutching the slippery
rock of our mother.

Your infant cries kneading her
addiction into submission. Your ample appetite and miniature
fingers keeping us spellbound.

I didn't know how to say it then
you belong to me
the way all newly arrived things belong
to the most ravenous.

I'm not speaking of her
hunger, the insatiable edges of it
demanding
our conspiratorial silence, slumbering away

our tiny blessings. Her naps smudging the house
into sullen and tiptoe and *shh*—tv on whisper, the two of us,
heads together, inches from the screen.

Say we grow and change into hoarders of light.
Say we grow and refuse the rock our leaving.
Say your thirst is what I sang to at night from my room

across the hall. Say I didn't know you were listening
when your five-year-old voice reached me.
Keep singing, you called. *Don't stop.*

LOVE

If not the word, then the stillness.
Let us linger here awhile.

If not the song, then the brushstroke.
Gentle. I am tender-headed.

This is how to love me,
with your hand holding the pain off at the root.

BREASTLESS

The nestle of fingers
            entwined with
                                        other fingers
            milk thistle   capsules breaking
                        open blood

                coagulating   pages of a book
                            unturned pigment-

            stained fingernails
                        bones losing
            density
                        a remembered song

                                        unsung
                                    stuck
    on a word   a thought
                things that have nothing

                                        in common

but the sound
                they don't make

loving a word

for itself   not

for its meaning:

crest-fallen
philistine
ingratiate

loving the meaning

but not the word:

pulchritude
bucolic
intercourse

sex

even that

nipples offering

themselves up

to tongue   to lips

to fingers

nipples that will never
offer

themselves up again—

like mine
words

whose sound and meaning
I love

and hate:

                    mamilla
                    teat
                    udder
                    licentious

the absurdity of everything
                    that doesn't make me

        salivate
        cum
        cackle
        moan

                    a paper towel soaked in turpentine
                    resting on the edge of a waste basket

        airing itself

        not combusting into flame not burning this place to the ground not this
hot flash not from sex or that novel about bondage everyone's read pages unturned inches
        and inches untouched   flammable   wickless   matchless.

ONCE AT AN ART PARTY IN CHELSEA

       a well-respected painter
told me I reminded him of a Gauguin.

I didn't ask him which. I knew
       what he meant. The women
were the same: brown, like me,

long black hair, like me. Topless.
       That was enough for him to slip
his hands into my otherness

and pull taut, tied up for future use.
       Today, all that Gauguin-island-girl-
hair is in a plastic bag on my floor

waiting to be donated so another
       woman will have something to cover
her bald as she waits for chemo

to dismantle her piece by piece.
       I wonder, Mr. Painter Man
if I sent it to you, would you paint

strands of me

into your next portrait?

My pubic hair,

my dark roots, could be her

eyebrows, her shadowing armpits.

You could swap her head for her pelvis

if you wanted to be more Picasso about it

and her pelvis for her

neck. Her neck for her ankle   ankle

for her toe toe   for her ear

ear for her neck   and pelvis

swap and swap   again and again   breasts

for her   breasts   for her   breasts

YEAR IN REVIEW

My mother told me two secrets this year,
both involving how a woman's body
can disguise its softest places.

The first anniversary of my father's death
passed without lit candle or prayer.

I forgot to remember him.

This is the truth of us.
I don't know where to hold my grief these days.
The world is turning in the wrong direction.

I am not what anyone thinks I am.

FATHER WEAVER

If he wasn't janitor he'd be gravel artist, he'd be glitter farmer, he'd groove skate
down beach hill to Isley Brothers. If he wasn't janitor he'd be tennis racketeer,
ocean tamer, cicada sequencer, he'd turn his knit cap upside down to catch fire

flies, load them into pitching machine, point upwards and shoot stars into sky.
If he hadn't been liquor undertaker, booze regulator, drunk-gambling-wish denier
he might have been daughter wrangler, fear whisperer, sweet lullaby impersonator.

His under-water voice might have sung me to float and swell. If he hadn't been vodka
foreman he might have used strands of daughter hair to draw maps of blackness
onto his back. I might have watched them stretch and curve and maze him into father

quest into secret daughter mission. I'd pack a flashlight and meals for the trip.
I'd stretch and nimble get. I'd compass take, whistle and song and song. I'd path
follow and lost get and around turn, around turn till I center reach and undead him.

CALL ME BY MY NAME

After the 2016 Presidential Election

Between Nina Simone's teeth and pendulum quiver—

> A tiny misery unfolds
> from the mountains and hills
> of America. Men with black
>
> lungs gather in red caps
> for their right to descend
> again. Polished white
>
> women give control
> of their wombs to a salmon-
> skinned savior for a myth.

Alternative fact: he will come for you too.

I'm the brown daughter
of a white woman who voted blue
and now has made a nest

called sorrow from twigs of left-
wing shame, from shards of blue
glass bottles and jellyfish,

from coral reef blue and eye bruise
blue, from her, there's plenty of room
for you blue, but how do I tell her

I can't live there? How do I
tell her she named me after papaya
flesh and cornhusk, after sweet

juice of Black women's song
whose only known border is water,
who dip sacramental bread in

Obeah chant? Slow churned
memories of the Arawak.
Did she know they were a poetic

people when she named me?
Did she prophecy the seeds of Ackee fruit
lingering in the ashen grooves

of my knees and elbows?
Their jerk and rock steady lilt.
What I don't know of them

is the white space of every page
I've not yet written. What I don't
know of my people is their name.

A tiny misery smokes meth
in the alluvial plains of stolen land.
Make America great

Again! slides through
willing teeth in the mouth
of last-ditch hope.

Alternative fact: I will fight for you too.

I'm the brown daughter
of a black man who died
like black men do: too soon,

back broke, inevitably. In
retrospect we should have
buried him in the worn down

beanie he wore every day—
yellow, green, and black.
Appropriation or premonition?

Were he here, he'd shrug, say,
ain't no surprise. Them white folk
never meant us t'have too much

slack in that rope. How do I tell him
I can't give up like that? How
do I tell him he named me

after a place designed to resist:
cocoa leaves and tamarind breeze,
cutlass slash and parish streets?

Did he know my name
would call attention to
how very American I am?

A tiny misery spreads
disease-like from every *he doesn't*
mean that, each *he tells it like it is,*

and *words are just words* I heard
from all the well-meaning
white folk who voted him

in. Between Standing Rock
and Flint, Michigan
—I am here.

Between refugee
and immigrant
—I am here.

Between birth control
and rape control
—I am here

Between Nina Simone's teeth
and pendulum quiver

WHAT'S BEEN CAGED

I thought *sieve* but said *shiv*.
I thought *blaspheme* but cursed anyway.
A good *fuck* said with conviction will knock the teeth out of rage.

I thought *convoluted* but said *convulsion*,
the uncontrollable movement behind the eyelids,
rapid, searching in the dark
hallways of history.

    We began the day like this,
    myself and I, arguing over the lyrics
    to *Passin' Me By*.

I wondered if they'd considered
the implications of "dopest Ethiopian."

    Myself thought my BA/MFA/PhD had PC'd the funk right out of me.
    It was a critical debate,
    an untheoretical contortion about imagination.
    Language, in theory, is representation
    (from the Latin *repreasentare*: to make present, set in view, display).

I sank my teeth into *exhibit*
to prove my point. The long history of grotesque exhibitions hung
before us. The word *hung* treed before us.

Language kept drawing arrows like this from word to slave to rape
to ancestor.

> Myself thought *survival*
> but said circumscribe (from the Latin *circumscribere*:
> to encircle, limit, restrain, confine).

I wanted another word to free us from the confines of survival.

> Myself did not say quiet but became it,
> as if the desire to rid myself of such limitations was asking
> too much. As if

I could only be one or the other:
myself or the I that contained myself, the words,
or the history that engendered them.

The arrows always return to what's been caged.
This time when thinking *incarceration*,

I said *sieve* (from the Old English *sife*: to pour out, drip, trickle),
like mourning I thought
but said revolution.

III.

even in death's hand
we fold the fingers up
and call them greens and
grow on them,
we hum them and make music.
call it our wildness then,
we are lost from the field
of flowers, we become
a field of flowers.

—LUCILLE CLIFTON

CELL REVOLT

My nose tells me things I don't want to believe,
how the morning air smells like hope.

My tongue told me, *crowds taste sour sometimes.*
That's what happens, I said, *when rage is left out in the sun*

to rot.

My skin is a suspicious organ.

Apparently what I see
in the faces of children is not really how they look. I said,
prophets only reveal themselves to the suffering.

My ears twist truths into similes before I'm able to hear them.
For example,

You are like the moon's surface.
When what they said was, *I don't understand you.*

My body tells me things I can't accept—
that cancer hasn't cured me. I closed my ears.

I did not want to touch its lies.

A MISEDUCATION

Brother, while you lined up snails on our linoleum floor
to create a path of slime through the house, I was learning
how a girl body bleeds without wounding. When you read
books about insects, reptiles, amphibians & mammals,
I watched films where girl animals were rescued by boy animals.
When you called me outside to show me what you found
beneath the rocks, I pretended to care. Years later you'd say,
it was my eyes that gave it away, how they darted about
as I feigned interest. You were learning to destroy things
and not get caught. I was learning how playing hard to catch
then becoming caught was the point. A distance of seven years.
I couldn't un-squirm myself long enough to kneel next to you
in the dirt, to dip my hands into the earth, delighted
with the mess, content not knowing what I'd find in the dark.

I watched you watching.
Of nature, this I recall—
a young boy. His heart.

WE WEREN'T A MURDER OR FLOCK

but a defense of girls
      bracing for impact.
She think, she all that don't she with her high-yella ass!
Iron gossip gutted into musculature.

The older girls carried knives
      and drew their eyebrows
      into thin dark arcs of war.

The telephone booth at Taco Bell
      we frequented. The useless torn wings
      we folded when Five-O rolled by
      prowling for truants—

      older boys moving
      from group home
      to juvy to our arms.

Our worries eclipsed by a replay of kisses.
The pollination of lips. The waiting.
The phone booth. He said he'd call at 2.
Give him 10 minutes. 10 minutes more.

In the observatory of mistakes we chipped our teeth
on stars trying to consume the night.

Walking to 7-11
his cheekbones glinting in cigarette light.
Fallen. Got my nose wide open.
My lonesome soothed

if only for the moment.

DANCING AT THE RUSH INN, CIRCA 1999

Sometimes it's a dive bar with a juke box
and whiskey.

Sometimes it's a slow dance
with a woman whose reckless body keeps you

sane and a murmur of strange
men who look but never

touch
and sometimes it's okay

to be a tease because tonight you just need
to feel hungered for
and you swear
you've seen galaxies in their eyes
and it makes you weightless

and the movement
of your hips tells a story you don't believe
but sometimes it isn't belief
it's muscle memory

the eight ball is still on the table
and your friend's tattoos

are still a threat
to the straight men
who stare but can't handle her pain

*

it must be enough

her cleavage
her smile
her drink-you-under-the-table
posture and when she takes
me in her arms I feel what's been
carved out of her. Our wounds meet and nothing
unlocks. We aren't healed

or even happy, but
for a moment we know
what power feels like.
We know what our bodies pressed
together like that conveys

but it's just a story we're telling because her man's coming
soon and I have another drink waiting

because galaxies can be treacherous
and I don't really like the song

we've been dancing to
till it ends.

SYMPHONIES

Buzzards circle overhead

when he touches the scarred surface. In this
        prophecy a body is strewn about
the empty streets, limbs dis-
        connected from carcass, a blood red

river flows outside its boundaries.
        This is where skin becomes tinted
or tainted. The origin of war paint
        has always been blood. The origin

of sex has always been need. When he touches
        what has not been touched in some time—
some equaling a number that takes itself
        too seriously, but also less than the number

of orgasms I've faked, which is to say,
        not seriously enough—I'll replace his silence
with an absence of symmetry. A cacophony,
        not like song at all, like the moments between

death and decay when bodies are ripe
        for the pulling and the picking and scavengers
unable to hide their lust call out to each other,
        staking their claim. Which cut has the sweetest

memories? They ca-caw and caw and caw.

        Although sex, for now, is that which came

before cancer, that is to say not a current

        dilemma, I miss what won't be there each time

a hand traces symphonies across my chest.

        I miss sex with that perfectly

worrisome body. The inches of waist–

        too many, the hips–too high, and breasts,

well, they had their own history.

A LANGUAGE SO FRAUGHT

I speak with many voices. Pristine and filthy,
dragging their tired chords through spilled blues.

Within each voice—a voice emerged, a voice subdued.
I don't know which is louder till they quiet. Even then.

The silence. Even then I am betrayed by how gluttonous
mine can be, hoarding words as a bowerbird hoards blue.

Sometimes I want to tame them, those greedy meaning makers.
Sometimes I question the kind of body that would lend itself

to such fantasy, that would acquiesce to a language so fraught
with violence and cunning. It has made me in the shape of silence.

It has left words to mold in my cage. Over and over again
I am written in a forgetful and more brutal language.

PORTRAIT OF A MOTHER WITH FIRE AND DESIRE

She softens her gullet
  for the swallowing.
All she wants is the honey.
The promise.
Her due.

Those she can't become, she consumes:
  a movie star, soul singer,
  philosopher, a priest. She'd pawn

her wolf inheritance for a standing ovation.
Her speech is a bar fight,
her balancing act, a confession.

She knows to desire a man
is in part
  a desire to be him,
  to be the pollen and the stamen,
  the seed and the soil,
  to leave her stinger behind
  in the sweetness before she dies.

LIKE A SOFT HORN

I saw through the evening,
a purple light.
The light held a sound.
I kept squinting at it trying to hear its octaves,
but all I heard were birds and so
I tried my wings, straightened my back
the way one does when attempting good posture
and did a little shimmy
to loosen them, but they wouldn't budge.

I could feel the constant pressure
between my shoulder blades.
It was painful
to hear the birds so full of flight and song,
but as I stood there

I thought about my mother's hunger
all those years ago
in college eating the goat's liver pulled straight
out of the animal's still warm body
when few of the other students would touch it,
not even, to the dismay of the teacher, the men.

Only two women
lifted the organ to their mouths
one after the other

wiping blood from their chins
smiling at how creature they'd become.

*

I want many things
and sometimes it's hard to hold
all this desire in one body.

If I had another body
that could store my desire,
a body that looked like me, but didn't
have the organs, muscles, and bones
taking up all the space, perhaps

my body, that is not me, would play
a series of songs
made up solely of the sounds of my future desire.
A mixtape of sorts,
but without titles or narrative arc.

The sound that would stand out the most
would be a rustling of leaves
like the rustle squirrels make playing at the base of trees,
but not exactly.

There would be more depth to it.
A wateriness.

Rustling water. Yes. Dry and wet, then
a chiming somewhere in the distance, not like bell chimes.
More like a soft horn,
like Coltrane

but also full of silence.
A horn chime full of silence.
And listening to this
mixtape of my desire that is to come,
I would think, *yes!*

This is a true thing.

And my body that is not me would turn,
a blinding purple.

STRING OF PEARLS

The string of pearls I bought for my deck last summer
have died for want of sun.
The parched plants now hang from the top of the fridge
reminding me of my ineptitude
each time my shoulder brushes a dried pearl to the floor.

My friend's father passed recently, succumbed to old age
and cancer. I remember
when I had mine, how she whisked me to her parents'
in Greenwich, how her frail father
took us on a boat on an inlet littered with yachts.

I thought then about the chemo coursing through me
killing cells indiscriminately,
the reckless and the rule-followers.

If my body now could talk to my body then, it would tell it
to jump, to join the old man
in the water, to let my bald head bob like a buoy,
to swim laps around the boats,
to not let what I've lost negotiate the terms of what I haven't.

You see, a few of the pearls have held on to their green.
For the first time
I think I understand—continuing on anyway is
a kind of forgiveness.
I get it now, why I refuse to let the plants go completely.

A CENTO FOR BLACK WOMEN WHO DIED FROM CANCER

- dedicated to Gwendolyn, Audre, Lorraine, Lucille, and June

Her bars lie wet, open and empty
        and she has made herself again
        out of flesh out of dictionaries.

I am she and this is my story
of Her.

        How much of the truth to tell?

      *

I was born black and female.

For those of us who were imprinted with fear
like a faint line in the center
of our foreheads, the dark hangs

heavily over the eyes. Nobody
show me how to make cup of coffee
with no hands.

      *

If I could grow arms on my scars
like them I wouldn't apologize for my thorns either.
Just stand in the desert
            and witness

the destruction
within me, hoping that

when the devil days
of my hurt drag out to their last
dregs and I resume on such legs as are left,
wondering—

which me will survive
all these liberations—

I might understand

except
that I am tired of understanding.

            *

If this alphabet could speak
its own tongue
it would be all symbol
surely.

Simply a long line—as in geometry,
you know, one that reaches
into infinity. And because we cannot see the end
we also cannot see

how it changes
in the non-cheering dark, in the many many mornings-
after; in the chalk and choke—

a huge raggedy scar.
And so I go on.

*

I wish to live
because life has within it

        that which is good,
        that which is beautiful,
        and that which is love.

*

Mama, I want so many things . . . I want so many things
that they are driving me kind of crazy

I cannot bear an interruption.
This is the shining joy;
the time of not-to-end.

I have decided

I have something to say
about female silence: so to speak
these are my 2c on the subject:

My work is to inhabit the silences
with which I have lived
and fill them with myself until
they have the sounds of the brightest day
and the loudest thunder.

*

. . . if anything should happen—
before 'tis done—may I trust
that all my commas and periods
will be placed and someone
will complete my thoughts

A BRIEF AND SORDID HISTORY OF THE SPECULUM

Dr. Sims's Use of Enslaved African Women as Experimental Subjects

Tell me Doctor Sims
how many women did it take?

In truth
you need not remember. You see
memory is what remains
in the tissue.

Intact.
Unmolested
by time and men and you
sir. We remember you.
                We carry your progress
in our blood,
passed down through generations
of women. Our ancestors'
rage rattles our cells.   This

is our cancer
sir. Confess.

What did you tell your children?
What memories
did they bequeath
to their sons?

No.
You need not explain.
I've seen it in their eyes,
these men I stumble into
going about my day—

know. Not in their minds,
but in their cells.

   They know
they've muscled their way into the deepest seas,
   parted them,
   played God for a while.

Sometimes when I look in their eyes
I see yours that held me

captive
on your table, naked,
legs pinned back
like a frog prepared
for dissection and when this happens

I'm certain
these men carry
your afflictions inside them.

If I pried them open, *doctor,*
believe me
they'd remember who I am.

AS THE NURSE FILLS OUT THE INTAKE FORM, THE OCEAN SPEAKS YOUR NAME

Golden Shovel after Gwendolyn Brooks

When the nurse asks, *have you ever been pregnant?*, I
clench my teeth, hold my breath for what comes next, *do you have
any children?* In the space between the questions I heard

the ocean sleep walking, followed it up the road where, in
the middle, under the streetlight, it turned around. The
mouth of the ocean spoke the names I never gave you, voices

I never learned by heart, a body I never held pacing the hallways of
motherhood pleading with God for solitude. In silence, the
nurse records my answers. I meet her silence with the wind

of my own quiet womb: the unbreathed who once visited, the
unboned who once trusted, the songs they never sang, their voices
never fading into sleep. I realize sorrow is not made solely of

this blood. Wind forgives the mother who opted out, but my-
sterious is the still childless woman who chose the same dim
impossible light. Listen, I wanted more joy to greet you, less time killed

in thirst, me—more woman able to take on the world for her children.

NATURALLY

Begin with a plant
then an animal. Move
your way up the chain of need
till you've learned enough
about sacrifice and scooping poop
to join the ranks of mother.

I have six eggs frozen
in a tube in New York.
Already these children
I may never have demand
from me monthly what
I have the least to give.

I remember the ritual of it.
Six days of pinched belly fat
and needles disappearing into skin,
my mother wincing because her hands
were causing her daughter pain.
Six days of driving to the hospital
for ultrasounds to determine
if my body was enough.

The nurse gossiping
about the young twenty-somethings
in the waiting room who weren't
getting chemo in a week,
who were there by choice
to preserve the youngest eggs possible,
whose parents were paying
thousands of dollars for them
to sit in a fertility clinic
on the Upper East Side defying age.

I haven't had the dream in a while,
the dream where I was running
from something and pregnant.
I can barely remember
the shape of the eagle,
her massive wings and the talons
that carried me to safety.

The doctors can't tell me
if I will do it naturally,
or at all, and I don't know
exactly what I want from this body.

PORTRAIT OF A MOTHER
WITH HAWK
AND HOUSE

Mother never decorated the house or planted a garden,
never placed the palm of her hand against the cool

surface of house, never said, *this we'll call home,*
never committed to being present, fixed. Immovable.

Never rooted herself in space and time, never stayed
but never left. Instead, floated like an apparition

through memory and stardust, recited stories of
blackouts, bruises, and bad decisions. Told them

with grin and cackle: how she preferred brutal to boring,
how she cursed with all her bones, how she demurred

only insofar as it got her closer to free, how she
gnashed her teeth when shushed or told to quiet,

how she dangled her rage towards men in front
of a daughter still dreaming of princes. How

there is not a hawk in the sky she won't point out,
not a willow branch she won't reach for, a melody

she won't sway to, an otter she won't meet at water's edge.
There is love and there is Love and there is LOVE

and I prefer the latter. This is how I take after her:
unwilling to become any small, watered-down thing.

UNRAVEL

My dad carried shame with him from Dallas
            to Oregon in '75, after Texas and the Army
            spit him out. The weight of it demanding
more than one syllable. *Sh-sh-shame*

like the deep baritone of his sorrow
            plucked into harmony when he was drunk
            doo-woping to Motown songs at the bar.
If I'd known that *correct speech* was hyperbole,

that my slippery S's weren't an impediment but
            part of his legacy, I may not have Sally-see-sawed
            my way through speech lessons till I could speak
right. Had I known right wasn't always a straight line,

that the mastectomy scar below my right breast
            if seen in the right light resembles a ripple
            on calm water after a heron takes flight, I might
have sought refuge in my inability to let go of sound's

repetitious comforts, rolling my tongue around
            each S till it stretched its long body out to bask
            in the light between my teeth, the way I bask
in the knowledge that my stutter wasn't mine

alone, the way I sometimes run my finger along
        the scar line wondering what it would feel like
        to live there, the way bra wires once lived there,
the way anticipation once lived there, the way

a lover's breath once held me captive, trembling.
        This ceremony of gestures. This ritual. This tenderness.
        I don't blame my father his absence, not fully.
He who un-sutured me with his constant leaving.

I know what a Black man whose father was
        a Black man, whose father was also a Black man,
        is made to endure here. I don't know
the pronunciation of his traumas, but I can feel them,

how easily they slip under my tongue, force
        my words to trip over themselves. During this
        havoc I sense him tending our legacy, just
as the doctors tended my wound—the kindness

of morphine, the anesthesiologist's sweet talk.
        After they stitched me up I knew there was more
        than an absence of tissue left inside. Sometimes
at night I can't help but search for a mistake,

an opening, a stutter of forgotten thread,
        something inarticulate to grab ahold of,
wrap my fingers around, to pull and pull and

                gently unravel me.

ABSENCE

I am learning to fill it slowly,
My hands deep in the earth.
I fancy myself a northern pitiful beast
Dazzled by the cold. But for now,
this heat is all I have. For now
I will walk through the flower fields
Reciting their names like a prayer
Or a plea: peony, hyacinth,
Crested cockscomb. *I found the dark honey*
Between the plague and its aftermath
Of more plague. What is suppressed
Always comes back stronger. I must admit,
I envy its flower-shaped resilience,
Such brilliant molecular beauty.
Soon we will learn to forage for dead things
On all fours tonguing tomorrow's ravages—
Blackened forests, oil-slick sea anemones,
A broken doll with a missing eye.
This is where I'll place the freshest bloom.
This is where I'll emerge from absence
Like a carnivorous creature after winter
Dripping with hunger.

NOTES

1. The Mary Szybist quote is from the poem "Invitation" from her book *Incarnadine.*
2. The quote from Suji Kwok Kim is from the poem "Translations from the Mother Tongue" in her book *Notes from a Divided Country.*
3. The poem "All That Splendor" is after the poem, "A Flight of Swiftlets Made Their Way In" by Vievee Francis from her book *Forest Primeval.*
4. The quote from Carl Phillips is taken from the poem "Seminar: Problems in Renaissance Painting" in his book *Cortège.*
5. The quote by Lucille Clifton is from her poem "Roots" in her book *good woman.*
6. The poem "A Language So Fraught" is a nod to Alejandra Pizarnik.
7. The poem "A Brief and Sordid History of the Speculum" addresses Dr. Sims, who was considered the father of gynecology. He had a statue in his honor in Central Park for decades. It was taken down due to protests in 2018.
8. The poem "A Cento for Black Women Who Died from Cancer" is an homage to Lucille Clifton, Audre Lorde, Gwendolyn Brooks, June Jordan, and Lorraine Hansberry. The lines used are from the following source material: "Good Woman" by Lucille Clifton; *June Jordan: Directed By Desire* by June Jordan; *Les Blancs: The Collected Last Plays*, "To Be Young Gifted and Black," "The American Negro Writer and His Roots: Toward a New Romanticism" and *A Raisin in the Sun* by Lorraine Hansberry; "A Litany for Survival," "Power," "Who Said It Was Simple," and *The Cancer Journals* by Audre Lorde; "Truth," "my dreams, my works, must wait till after hell," "To Prisoners," "An Aspect of Love, Alive in the Ice and Fire," "Still Do I Keep My Look, My Identity . . ." by Gwendolyn Brooks.
9. The poem "As the Nurse Fills Out the Intake Form, the Ocean Speaks Your Name" is a Golden Shovel with a line from a Gwendolyn Brooks poem.
10. The line from Pablo Neruda in the poem "Absence" is from his poem "Sonnet xxx."
11. "Passin' Me By" in the poem "What's Been Caged" is the title of a song by Pharcyde.

ACKNOWLEDGMENTS

Grateful acknowledgement is made to the editors and staff of the following publications in which some of these poems first appeared, sometimes in a different format or a different title:

Rattle: "Call Me By My Name"

Seattle Review of Books: "Boneless"

Third Coast Magazine: "All That Splendor"

Hayden's Ferry: "Far From Grace"

Jack Straw Anthology: "Year in Review"

Chatwin Books: "No Other Language"

San Miguel de Allende Writing Conference Contest Winner, 2019: "Teaching the Beasts to Devour My Mother"

December Magazine: "What Remains"

The Inspired Poet edited by Susan Landgraf, Two Sylvias Press: "A Brief and Sordid History of the Speculum" and "Cell Revolt"

Glass Poetry: "Unravel"

The Missouri Review: "Forbidden" and "Once At An Art Party in Chelsea"

The Massachusetts Review: "Naturally"

RHINO Poetry: "Father Weaver" and "Breastless"

Ruminate: "As the Nurse Fills Out the Intake Form, the Ocean Speaks Your Name"

Indiana Review: "The End of Sorrow Is Not Happiness"

DIAGRAM: "What's Been Caged"

Poetry Northwest: "Portrait of a Mother with Hawk and House," "Film Script: On An Open Road (an anti-drama)," and "Like a Soft Horn"

Hunger Mountain: "Neglectus"

Prairie Schooner: "Symphonies"

Expedition Press: "Love" as letterpress broadside

GRATITUDE

To the mentors and professors who nudged me ever closer to this identity called poet, I hope you know how necessary you were: Dorianne Laux, Vievee Francis, Ellen Bass, Hope Wabuke. Special thanks to the late Marvin Bell, who helped me believe in my own poetic instincts. And of course, a big thank you to the indominable Kwame Dawes, whose mentorship and, I dare say, friendship has shown me that the life of a poet is more than just the writing on the page, but is also the editing, championing, advancing, and gathering of voices. I am a citizen of poetry because of you.

To my poets in arms who helped me shape this thing called a book, your time, care, and attention were invaluable: *the frustration of poets* and my first readers—Jennifer Saunders, Craig Van Rooyen, Michele Bombardier, Nancy Gomez, and Rebecca Patrascu; my Nebraska peeps—Katie Marya, Ava Winter, Saddiq Dzukogi, and Jess Poli, thank you! I am indebted to my early inspirations: Laurie Guerrero, who showed me what a poet could be before I even knew that I was one; Seamus Scanlon for being my first true writer friend; Kevin Quashie whose compassion and grace as a teacher helped me fall deeper in love with literature.

To KMA Sullivan and YesYes Books, I appreciate the hours long conversations we had about each line and caesura and the publication process in general. Your vision and attention to detail were invaluable. Gratitude to Alban Fisher for the beautiful cover design and artist Portia Svavahera for the cover art.

Thank you to the following friends, organizations, and institutions that read, championed, supported, promoted, and/or offered spaces of silence and community that enabled me to write the next word and the word after that: Jack Straw Writers, Hugo House, Jourdan Imani Keith, Jane Wong, Anastacia Renee, Hedgebrook, Seattle

Arts and Lectures, Pacific University, and The University of Nebraska-Lincoln, especially Stacey Waite.

To my family and friends for their ongoing support and inspiration: Alfred and Gladys for your love and constancy; Geneva and Al, thanks for your consistent presence at my early readings when I was a terrified baby poet; Carla for the hours upon hours of conversations about poetry, family, love, loss, and MFA'ing (We did the thang!); Leslie and Melinda for your enthusiasm and for welcoming me to the strange new place called the Midwest; Jessica and Endeliza, I wouldn't have made it here without your friendship these past thirty plus years; Laura for your heart and for being my rock when I needed it the most.

Alfred, dear brother, you inspire me every day. I want to be like you when I grow up. Or as the wise one said, *The force is strong with this one.*

And mom, well, what can I say. You have always been and will always be my ocean and everything above it.

To little brown girls and teenage girls, to rageful and grief-full women, to cancer survivors and misogyny survivors, to all mothers and daughters, this book is for you.

JAMAICA BALDWIN (she/her) is a poet and educator originally from Santa Cruz, CA. Her debut collection, *Bone Language*, was released in 2023 by YesYes Books. Her work has appeared in *Guernica*, *World Literature Today*, *The Adroit Journal*, and *The Missouri Review*, among others. Her accolades include a 2023 Pushcart Prize, 2021 National Endowment for the Arts Fellowship, the 2021 RHINO Poetry editor's prize, and winner of the 2019 San Miguel de Allende Writer's Conference Contest in Poetry. Her writing has been supported by Hedgebrook, Furious Flower, and the Jack Straw Writers program. Jamaica is currently the associate editor of *Prairie Schooner* at the University of Nebraska–Lincoln where she is pursuing her PhD in English with a focus on poetry and Women's and Gender Studies.

ALSO FROM YESYES BOOKS

FICTION

Girls Like Me by Nina Packebush

Three Queerdos and a Baby by Nina Packebush

WRITING RESOURCES

Gathering Voices: Creating a Community-Based Poetry Workshop
by Marty McConnell

FULL-LENGTH COLLECTIONS

Ugly Music by Diannely Antigua

Cataloguing Pain by Allison Blevins

Gutter by Lauren Brazeal Garza

What Runs Over by Kayleb Rae Candrilli

This, Sisyphus by Brandon Courtney

40 WEEKS by Julia Kolchinsky Dasbach

Salt Body Shimmer by Aricka Foreman

Forever War by Kate Gaskin

Ceremony of Sand by Rodney Gomez

Undoll by Tanya Grae

Loudest When Startled by luna rey hall

Everything Breaking / For Good by Matt Hart

Sons of Achilles by Nabila Lovelace

Landscape with Sex and Violence by Lynn Melnick

Refusenik by Lynn Melnick

GOOD MORNING AMERICA I AM HUNGRY AND ON FIRE by jamie mortara

Stay by Tanya Olson

a falling knife has no handle by Emily O'Neill

Another Way to Split Water by Alycia Pirmohamed

To Love An Island by Ana Portnoy Brimmer

One God at a Time by Meghan Privitello

I'm So Fine: A List of Famous Men & What I Had On by Khadijah Queen

If the Future Is a Fetish by Sarah Sgro

Gilt by Raena Shirali

Say It Hurts by Lisa Summe

Boat Burned by Kelly Grace Thomas

Helen Or My Hunger by Gale Marie Thompson

As She Appears by Shelley Wong

RECENT CHAPBOOK COLLECTIONS

Vinyl 45s

   Inside My Electric City by Caylin Capra-Thomas

   Exit Pastoral by Aidan Forster

   Of Darkness and Tumbling by Mónica Gomery

   The Porch (As Sanctuary) by Jae Nichelle

   Juned by Jenn Marie Nunes

   Unmonstrous by John Allen Taylor

   Preparing the Body by Norma Liliana Valdez

   Giantess by Emily Vizzo